Library

by Ann Morgan

Photographs by Dan Wopperer

Easy
Stuff
Library

STARTING GATE PRESS

This series is dedicated to the loving memories of our mothers,
Maureen Cotter Morgan and Dorothy Coleman Wopperer

The author and illustrator would like to extend their heartfelt thanks to the following people for their enduring enthusiasm and encouragement for this project, as well as for their professional expertise:

Nicole Wopperer and Eric Willis, IT design and layout, RareEdge Design Group
Patrice Morgan, MBA
Susan Stonesifer, Glenwood Library; Howard County, Maryland
Janet Lasky
The Morgan Girls – Putt, Peggy, Susan, Patrice
The Wopperer Girls – Christy, Nicole, Jan, Erin
Ellen Morgan Rose and Peter
Anne Tatem
Glenwood Library Staff
Wood Library Staff; Canandaigua, NY
Chili Public Library; Chili, NY
School Media Centers –
  TJ Connor Elementary; Scottsville, NY
  Christ the King Elementary School; Snyder, NY

Text copyright 2005, by Ann Morgan, M.Ed.
Photographic illustrations copyright 2005, Dan Wopperer, M.D.

First Edition
Library of Congress Cataloging-in-Publication Date
10 9 8 7 6 5 4 3 2

Morgan, Ann. Library/ by Ann Morgan, photographs by Dan Wopperer

Summary: The features and functions of a public library are described in simple text for emerging readers and speakers of the English language, with vivid supporting photographic illustrations.

ISBN 0-9773253-490000
Easy Stuff Library (ESL) Series
Starting Gate Press - startinggatepress.com
Printed and bound in Canada by Friesens of Altona, Manitoba

Table of Contents

Word Help – Before You Read

Words to Practice

library	videotape	check out
listen	audio books	counter
borrow	recorded books	slots
return	audiotapes	book drop
patron	languages	shelves
card	foreign	shelf
sections	computers	stacks
information	printers	book truck
reference	librarian	cart
newspapers	alphabetical order	display
magazines	numerical order	spinner
periodicals	circulation	

Word Help

More Words to Practice

Plural Words

one library	two or more libraries
one child	two or more children
one person	two or more people
one story	two or more stories
one shelf	two or more shelves

Compound Words

cannot	=	can + not
something	=	some + thing
newspaper	=	news + paper
sometimes	=	some + times
outside	=	out + side

Possessive Word

children	children's

Introduction

A library is a place to get things to read. Libraries have many books. Libraries have things to listen to. Libraries have things to help you do work. Libraries have things to help you have fun. You can do many things at the library.

At the Library

You do not buy things from a library. You borrow things from a library.
You can take things home when you borrow them. A library worker tells you
when to give the things back. You return things when you give them back.
A person who uses the library is a library patron.

You need a library card to borrow things from the library. You can borrow books from the library. You can borrow movies from the library. You can borrow music from the library. You get a library card at the library. A person who works at the library gives you a library card. You use a library card to borrow things from the library.

Libraries have tables and chairs. You can sit and read. You can sit and talk. You can sit and write. You can sit and work. You do not need a library card to use tables and chairs at the library.

Sections

Most libraries have many things to look at or listen to. Things that are the same are in the same part of the library. The parts of the library are sections. Libraries have many sections.

Libraries have books for children. Books for children are in the children's section. You can borrow books from the children's section. You can use your library card to get things from the children's section.

Some things stay at the library. You cannot take them home. You use them at the library. You do not need a library card to use some things at the library.

Libraries have books with information. Information is what you want to know about something. Books with information are reference books. Reference books are in the reference section. You cannot take reference books out of the library.

Libraries have newspapers and magazines. Newspapers and magazines are periodicals. They are in the periodical section. You cannot take newspapers and magazines out of the library.

Libraries have movies. The movies are on videotape or DVD. Movies are
in the movie section. You can use your library card to borrow movies from the
library.

Libraries have books you can hear. Books you can hear are audio books.
Audio books are recorded books. They are in the audio book section. You do
not read audio books. You listen to audio books. You can borrow audio books
from the library.

Libraries have music. The music is on CDs or audiotapes. They are in the music section. The music section has different places for different kinds of music. You can borrow music from the library.

Libraries have books with very big letters. Books with very big letters are large print books. They are in the large print book section. Large print books are for people who cannot see well. You can borrow large print books from the library.

Libraries have books in many languages. Books that are not in English are in the foreign language section. You can borrow foreign language books from the library.

Libraries have computers. You can work on the computers. You can play on the computers. You can write things on the computers. Some computers have special programs for children.

The library has printers. Printers take words from the computers. Printers put the words on paper. You can take the paper home. You cannot borrow computers from the library. Sometimes you need a library card to use the printers and the computers in a library.

Librarians

People work at the library. A person who works at the library is a librarian. Librarians help you at the library. The librarian at the Information Desk tells you about things in the library. The librarian at the Information Desk helps you find things at the library.

Librarians put things away. Things at the library have to go in the right places. Some things go in the same order as the English alphabet. Some things go in ABC order. ABC order is alphabetical order. Librarians use the names of the writers to put books in alphabetical order.

Some things at the library have numbers. Things with numbers are in number order. Number order is numerical order. The librarian uses the numbers to put things away in numerical order.

Some librarians work in the children's section. Librarians in the children's section read stories to children at the library. Librarians in the children's section take care of the books and toys.

Some librarians work at the Circulation Desk. The Circulation Desk is the Check Out Desk. You borrow things at the Circulation Desk. The librarian at the Circulation Desk checks things out for you. The Circulation Desk is flat on top. The flat part is a counter. You put things on the counter for the librarian. You give your library card to the librarian.

You return things at the Circulation Desk. You can give your things back to the librarian. You can return things in special places at the Circulation Desk. You return things in the return slots. You put your things in the return slots.

You can return things if the library is not open. You can return things in special places outside the library. You can put things in the outside book drop. A librarian takes your things from the book drop. A librarian puts them away.

Shelves

Libraries have shelves. Shelves are flat places that have things on them. One shelf is over another shelf in the library. There are many shelves in the library. You can walk next to the shelves. You can take what you want off the shelves.

Many shelves are next to more shelves. Shelves next to more shelves are stacks. Most stacks are big. Libraries have stacks.

Some things in the library are not in the stacks. Some things are on small shelves with wheels. A small shelf with wheels is a book truck or a cart. You can borrow things from book trucks and carts.

Some things in the library are on tables. Some things are on top of the stacks. They are on display. Things on display are easy to see. You can borrow things on display.

Some things in the library are on shelves that go around. Shelves that go around are on a spinner. You can borrow things from spinners.

Summary

A library has many things for you to look at or listen to. Libraries have sections. You can borrow things from a library. You can use some things only at the library. Librarians help you at the library. Things in libraries have to be put away in the right places. You can do many things at the library.

More Pictures

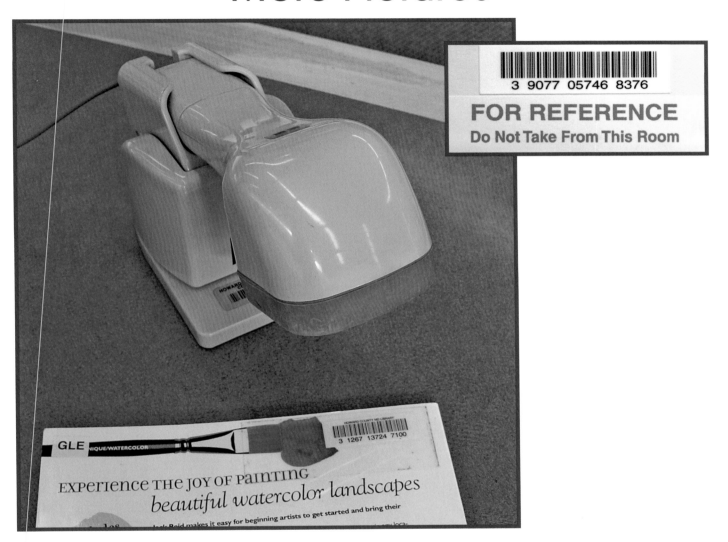

FOR REFERENCE
Do Not Take From This Room

A scanner uses barcodes to put book information into a computer.

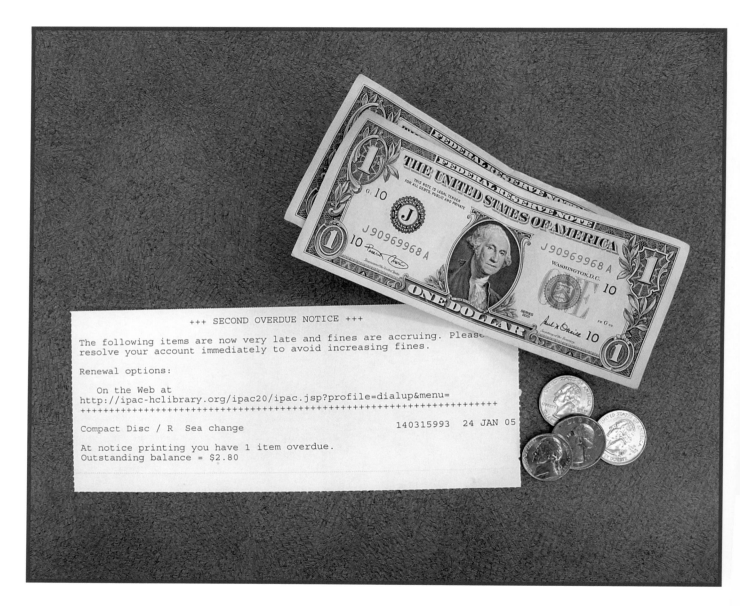

An overdue fine is money you give to the library when you return something late.

A copy machine makes more pages of paper you already have.

A study carrel and a study room are quiet places where you can work alone.

Some libraries have places where people can work together.

Some small books help you study and learn about other, bigger books.

A series is a set of books that go together.

A tutor gives a student extra help with schoolwork.

You can read to a friend at the library.

Some children's sections have toys and small tables and chairs.

The library staff is all the people who work at the library.

Book Talk – After You Read

1. Tell where things are on display in the library.

2. Who helps you at the library?

3. Tell what a book truck is.

4. What is numerical order?

5. Draw a picture of library stacks.

6. Tell someone how to borrow a book from the library.

7. Tell why things in the library have to be put away in the right places.

8. Look at the "More Pictures" pages. Look at three things. Tell what library sections those things go in.

9. Think about going to the library to get information. Tell one way you can get information and take it home.

10. Draw a picture of the inside of a library. Draw five things or more. Label them.

11. You cannot check out reference books. Do you think this is good or bad? Tell why.

12. Tell four things you think all libraries need for patrons. Tell why you think those things are important.